It's Diwali!

by Richard Sebra

BUMBA BOOKS™

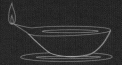

LERNER PUBLICATIONS ◆ MINNEAPOLIS

Note to Educators:

Throughout this book, you'll find critical thinking questions. These can be used to engage young readers in thinking critically about the topic and in using the text and photos to do so.

Lerner Publications Company
A division of Lerner Publishing Group, Inc.
241 First Avenue North
Minneapolis, MN 55401 USA

For reading levels and more information, look up this title at www.lernerbooks.com.

Library of Congress Cataloging-in-Publication Data

Names: Sebra, Richard, 1984- author.
Title: It's Diwali! / by Richard Sebra.
Description: Minneapolis : Lerner Publications, [2017] | Series: Bumba books—It's a holiday! | Includes
    bibliographical references and index.
Identifiers: LCCN 2016018683 (print) | LCCN 2016027409 (ebook) | ISBN 9781512425635 (lb : alk. paper) |
    ISBN 9781512429213 (pb : alk. paper) | ISBN 9781512427424 (eb pdf)
Subjects: LCSH: Divali—Juvenile literature.
Classification: LCC BL1239.82.D58 S43 2017 (print) | LCC BL1239.82.D58 (ebook) | DDC 294.5/36—dc23

LC record available at https://lccn.loc.gov/2016018683

Manufactured in the United States of America
1 – VP – 12/31/16

LERNER
SOURCE

Expand learning beyond the printed book. Download free, complementary educational resources for this book from our website, www.lerneresource.com.

Table of Contents

Diwali 4

Diwali Diyas 22

Picture Glossary 23

Index 24

Read More 24

Diwali

Diwali is an Indian holiday.

It happens in October

or November.

Many people in India celebrate Diwali. Diwali is India's most important holiday.

What important holidays does your family celebrate?

Diwali is also called the Festival of Lights.

Lights are an important part of the holiday.

People light small oil lamps.

Why is Festival of Lights another good name for Diwali?

Diwali lasts five nights.

People decorate the first two days.

They put up lights.

The third day is the

most important.

People dress up.

They gather with family.

They say special prayers.

14

Fireworks light up the sky.

People get together to watch.

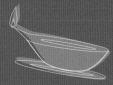

Then people have a big feast with family.

They eat sweet treats too.

What other holidays include a big feast?

The holiday has two
more days.
People stay with family
and friends.
People give gifts
to each other.

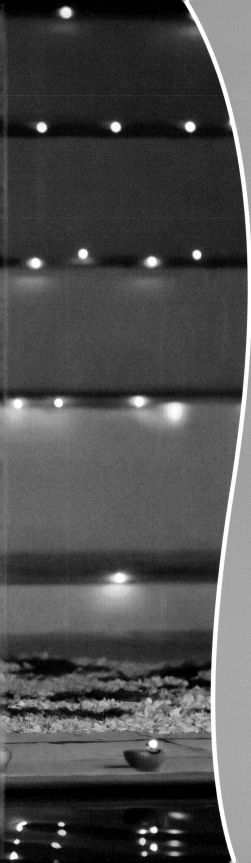

Diwali is a time

to be happy.

It is a celebration

of good things in life.

Diwali Diyas

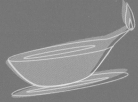

A diya is a small oil lamp. Diyas are usually made of clay. To celebrate Diwali, people light the wicks of the diyas.

Picture Glossary

decorate

to put up special and pretty things for a holiday

feast

a large meal

fireworks

devices that explode to make loud noises and colorful lights

prayers

words people say or think to their god

23

Index

feast, 16

Festival of Lights, 8

fireworks, 15

gifts, 19

India, 7

lights, 8, 11

nights, 11

prayers, 12

treats, 16

Read More

Chopra, Shweta. *The Diwali Gift.* Belmont, CA: 3 Curious Monkeys, 2015.

Pettiford, Rebecca. *Diwali.* Minneapolis: Bullfrog Books, 2015.

Sebra, Richard. *It's Easter!* Minneapolis: Lerner Publications, 2017.

Photo Credits